T0375044

The Carver Policy Governance Guide Series

The Policy Governance Model and the Role of the Board Member
A Carver Policy Governance Guide, Revised and Updated

Ends and the Ownership
A Carver Policy Governance Guide, Revised and Updated

The Governance of Financial Management
A Carver Policy Governance Guide, Revised and Updated

Adjacent Leadership Roles: CGO and CEO
A Carver Policy Governance Guide, Revised and Updated

Evaluating CEO and Board Performance
A Carver Policy Governance Guide, Revised and Updated

Implementing Policy Governance and Staying on Track
A Carver Policy Governance Guide, Revised and Updated

Praise for the Policy Governance Model

"Reading these guides is a great way to start your journey towards excellence in governance. All the essentials are there, short but clear. And these six guides will also prove to be an excellent GPS device along the way."

>—Jan Maas, PG consultant, Harmelen, The Netherlands

"The guides are a great way to introduce busy board members to the basic principles of Policy Governance. Their bite-size approach is inviting, covering the entire model, albeit in less detail, without overwhelming the reader. They are succinct and easy to read, including practical points of application for board members. Consultants asked to recommend initial reading about the model can do no better than these guides."

>—Jannice Moore, president, The Governance Coach™,
>Calgary, Canada

"Boards introduced to Policy Governance quickly become hungry for information but are short on time. These guides help board members quickly absorb the key principles of the Policy Governance model. They are invaluable."

>—Sandy Brinsdon, governance consultant,
>Christchurch, New Zealand

"For some board leaders the governance elephant is best eaten one bite at a time. The Carver Policy Governance Guide series provides a well-seasoned morsel of understanding in a portion that is easily digested."

>—Phil Graybeal, Ed.D., Graybeal and Associates, LLC,
>Greer, South Carolina

"Would you or your board benefit from a quick overview of essential governance concepts from the world's foremost experts on the topic, John and Miriam Carver? Thanks to their new six-booklet series, you can quickly familiarize or refresh yourself with the principles that make Policy Governance the most effective system of governance in existence. These booklets are the perfect solution for board members who are pressed for time but are dedicated to enhancing their own governance skills."

>—Dr. Brian L. Carpenter, CEO, National Charter
>Schools Institute, United States

CARVER
POLICY GOVERNANCE®
GUIDE

Adjacent Leadership Roles:
CGO and CEO

Revised and Updated

JOHN CARVER
MIRIAM CARVER

JOSSEY-BASS
A Wiley Imprint
www.josseybass.com

Published by Jossey-Bass
A Wiley Imprint
One Montgomery, Ste. 1200, San Francisco, CA 94104   www.josseybass.com

Library of Congress Cataloging-in-Publication Data

Carver, John.
  Adjacent leadership roles: CGO and CEO: a Carver policy governance guide / John Carver and Miriam Carver. —Rev. and updated ed.
    p. cm. —(The Carver policy governance guide series)
  ISBN 978-0-470-39255-3 (alk. paper)
  1. Boards of directors. 2. Chief executive officers. 3. Directors of corporations. 4. Corporate governance. I. Carver, Miriam Mayhew. II. Title.
  HD2745.C3667 2009
  658.4'21—dc22

                                                                           2009003148

REVISED AND UPDATED EDITION
HB Printing   10 9 8 7 6 5 4 3 2

Y ou've heard the titles: Chair, CEO, Chair and CEO, President, Executive Vice President, General Manager, Lead Director, Secretary General, Chief Governance Officer, Executive Director, and on and on. What are the roles that go with these titles? What responsibilities and accountabilities do the title holders have to live up to? Do all these titles mean the same thing?

In this Carver Policy Governance Guide, we examine the leadership roles needed in the boardroom and the executive suite by Policy Governance boards. We identify two important and separate functions that are key to enabling both governance and management to have the benefit of optimal leadership. These functions are performed by the positions we will call CGO and CEO, though each may be given any of a wide variety of titles like those above.

To begin this look at board and executive leadership, we review the Policy Governance model explained in the Carver Policy Governance Guide titled *The Policy Governance Model and the Role of the Board Member*. This review will be brief, and if you are unsure of the points referenced here, reading that Guide or any of the other publications explaining the Policy Governance model will be helpful.

Policy Governance in a Nutshell

- The board exists to act as the informed voice and agent of the owners, whether they are owners in a legal or moral sense. All owners are stakeholders but not all stakeholders are owners, only those whose position in relation to an organization is equivalent to the position of shareholders in a for-profit corporation.

- The board is accountable to owners that the organization is successful. As such, it is not advisory to staff but an active link in the chain of command. All authority in the staff organization and in components of the board flows from the board.

- The authority of the board is held and used as a body. The board speaks with one voice in that instructions are expressed by the board as a whole. Individual board members have no authority to instruct staff.

- The board defines in writing its expectations about the intended effects to be produced, the intended recipients of those effects, and the intended worth (cost-benefit or priority) of the effects. These are *Ends policies*. All decisions made about effects, recipients, and worth are *ends* decisions. All decisions about issues that do not fit the definition of ends are *means* decisions. Hence in Policy Governance, means are simply not ends.

- The board defines in writing the job results, practices, delegation style, and discipline that make up its own job. These are board means decisions, categorized as *Governance Process policies* and *Board-Management Delegation policies*.

- The board defines in writing its expectations about the means of the operational organization. However, rather than prescribing board-chosen means—which would enable the CEO to escape accountability for attaining ends—these policies define limits on operational means, thereby placing boundaries on the authority granted to the CEO. In effect, the board describes those means that would be unacceptable even if they were to work. These are *Executive Limitations policies*.

- The board decides its policies in each category first at
the broadest, most inclusive level. It further defines
each policy in descending levels of detail until reaching
the level of detail at which it is willing to accept any
reasonable interpretation by the applicable delegatee of
its words thus far. Ends, Executive Limitations, Governance Process, and Board-Management Delegation
policies are exhaustive in that they establish control
over the entire organization, both board and staff. They
replace, at the board level, more traditional documents
such as mission statements, strategic plans, and budgets.

- The identification of any delegatee must be unambigu-
ous as to authority and responsibility. No subparts of
the board, such as committees or officers, can be given
jobs that interfere with, duplicate, or obscure the job
given to the CEO.

- More detailed decisions about ends and operational
means are delegated to the CEO if there is one. If there
is no CEO, the board must delegate to two or more delegatees, avoiding overlapping expectations or causing
disclarity about the authority of the various managers.
In the case of board means, delegation is to the CGO
unless part of the delegation is explicitly directed else-
where, for example, to a committee. The delegatee has
the right to use any reasonable interpretation of the
applicable board policies.

- The board must monitor organizational performance
against previously stated Ends policies and Executive
Limitations policies. Monitoring is only for the purpose
of discovering if the organization achieved a reasonable
interpretation of these board policies. The board must
therefore judge the CEO's interpretation, rationale for

its reasonableness, and the data demonstrating the accomplishment of the interpretation. The ongoing monitoring of the board's Ends and Executive Limitations policies constitutes the CEO's performance evaluation.

Empowering Parallel Leaders: CGO and CEO

In a way, we could say that the board has two employees, though in nonprofit organizations and some governmental organizations one of them is usually unpaid. Both the CEO (by whatever title the board chooses) and the CGO (also by whatever title the board chooses) exist to see to it that some part of the board's expectation is carried out. You can see that it is important that the board make sure that the jobs of these two officers do not overlap. When supervisors of any sort, including boards, have more than one person working for them, carefully separating the functions of the subordinates is crucial. If you don't have a clear job, it's hard for your boss to hold you clearly accountable. You may not mind this, but the boss should mind very much, as poor performance ultimately reflects on him or her.

In Policy Governance, the two officers who report to the board are carefully described and their functions separated. We'll start our discussion of this by looking at Figure 1.

In Figure 1, you see that decisions about Ends, Executive Limitations, Governance Process, and Board-Management Delegation can be arranged to form a circle, organized from the broadest to the more narrow levels in the "mixing bowl" or nested-set manner. In effect, the board has encircled the organization, including the board itself, with its policies. It is in control of all issues at the broad levels, while specifics about those issues are left to others to decide. While individuals and even non–board members will frequently play a role in the board's reaching the decisions that create these broad policies, decisions to adopt this or that policy language belong only to the board itself.

Figure 1. The Policy Circle.

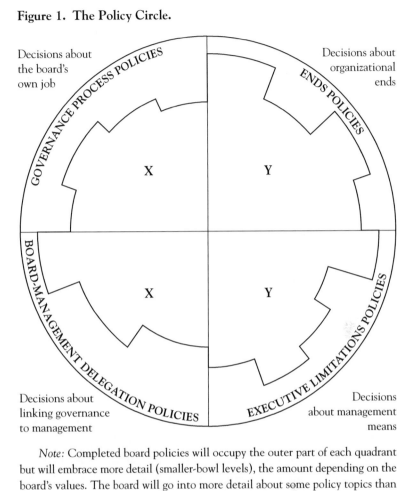

Decisions about the board's own job

GOVERNANCE PROCESS POLICIES

Decisions about organizational ends

ENDS POLICIES

X

Y

BOARD-MANAGEMENT DELEGATION POLICIES

X

Y

EXECUTIVE LIMITATIONS POLICIES

Decisions about linking governance to management

Decisions about management means

Note: Completed board policies will occupy the outer part of each quadrant but will embrace more detail (smaller-bowl levels), the amount depending on the board's values. The board will go into more detail about some policy topics than others, even within a given quadrant. Notice that the quadrant containing all staff means issues will be addressed by the board in a constraining or negative fashion (hence the policy category titled "executive limitations"). Empty space in the middle represents smaller decisions that the board is content to leave to delegatees. The CGO will be given authority to make decisions in the spaces marked X. (Foreshadowing later discussion of this role, CGO is used to indicate the chief governance officer, a function normally fulfilled by the board chair.) The CEO will be given authority to make decisions in the space marked Y.

The effect of these broad policies in each of the four policy categories is to initiate a cascading flow of decisions matched with equally cascading delegation of authority. When the board has described its expectations to the "any reasonable interpretation" point, its delegatees are then authorized to make all further decisions, as long as they can be shown to be reasonable interpretations. The board is thus fulfilling its leadership role by setting the organizational stage for carefully framed decision authority throughout. You are probably used to hearing that the board is the "final authority," but as you can tell, the flow of decision making from the board to others means that in a very real and concrete way, the Policy Governance board is instead the "initial authority."

Derivation of the CGO-CEO Role Distinction

So, built on the board's work of creating a few very high-leverage policies, authority is passed on to the CGO and the CEO, each cleanly separated from the other by being in two separate domains, as illustrated by the left and right sides of the circle, respectively, in Figure 1. From Figure 1, we can infer an important characteristic of the roles of these two officers: each has authority to make decisions, but always below the board's authority and therefore controlled by board decisions. That is, each works for the board, not the reverse. We can tell that about each role, but exactly what performance is expected in each role is defined by the content of the applicable board policies—the policy decisions expressed by the board, for the CGO, in Governance Process and Board-Management Delegation policies and, for the CEO, in Ends and Executive Limitations policies. That policy content will differ from board to board and even in the same board over time.

Therefore, in a given organization with a specific CGO and CEO, although we can understand where each fits in the scheme of things (their roles), concrete performance expectations for these roles are not defined until the board has done its job first. This contrasts with conventional wisdom in which boards seem quite comfortable creating a job description for the CEO when they have failed to define what the organization is to produce. In other words, boards try to define their CEO's job when they have not only not done their own job but have not even decided what their own job covers.

That commonplace anomaly is made possible by the long-standing tradition of defining a job by its activities rather than its results. For example, defining the CEO's job as "to manage the organization" or "to oversee the organization" is not uncommon, but it obscures the fact that there is no expected outcome in the definition. Defining the CGO's job as "to chair the board" or "to communicate with the CEO" similarly falls into what has been called the activity trap: treating a prescribed activity as if it is the result the activity was meant to achieve.

As to the CEO's job—demonstrated on the right side of the circle—when the board in making policy has reached its "any reasonable interpretation" point, the CEO is authorized to make, cause to be made, and be accountable to the board for all remaining decisions and actions. The "any reasonable interpretation" point is that level of detail in policymaking after which the board is willing to accept any reasonable interpretation of what policy says to that point. Hence we can see that the CEO is accountable to the board for the performance of all of the organization below the board, and the performance for which he or she is accountable is fulfillment of any reasonable interpretation of the board's Ends and Executive Limitations policies.

As to the CGO's job—demonstrated on the left side of the circle—when the board in making policy has reached its "any reasonable interpretation" point, the CGO is authorized to make, cause to be made, and be accountable to the board for all further decisions and actions. The CGO is accountable not that the board performs, since all members of the board share that accountability, but that the board is led in such a way that it is always aware of and following the performance standards that it set for itself. Leading in that way requires that the CGO give careful attention to issues of group process. It also requires the CGO to have the courage to confront the board with its own departure from its commitments. And it requires the CGO to be unafraid to make the decisions he or she has been authorized to make, since failure to use legitimately granted authority is actually an abuse of authority. CGOs must be decisive in the leadership the board has asked of them.

Both the CEO and the CGO are empowered officers. Each has the right and the obligation to make decisions. That is very different from the right to ask permission to make decisions. But the decisions they make must be reasonable interpretations of the policies in their specific domain. You can see that the areas in which they have authority have been carefully separated so the roles do not overlap. Overlapping the roles of the CEO and the CGO inevitably causes confusion at best and a power struggle at worst.

> So if you are a board member, a power struggle between a CGO and CEO is a board problem, not a CGO-CEO problem. It means the board either failed to separate the roles or tolerates violation of that separation by one or both.

The CGO does not have authority or responsibility on the right side of the circle, as this is the CEO's domain. The CEO can scarcely be held accountable by the board for the operation of this domain if his or her authority and choices can be overruled by the CGO.

Similarly, the CEO does not have authority or responsibility on the left side of the circle, though it is common practice for traditional boards to act as if their CEO is responsible for the board's quality of governance. In Policy Governance, the CEO does not stage-manage the board by being responsible for producing its agenda or arranging its education and input mechanisms. If the board cannot govern itself, it cannot govern an organization.

You may have noticed that occasionally the media will report high-profile situations in which the CEO and the chair of a corporation or prominent nonprofit have been unable to settle the matter of who has what authority, and the situation has ended in a firing, a court case, or both. Combine these stories with the fact that the roles of CGO and CEO are often merged in corporate boards, and you have plenty of illustrations that traditional boards have not figured out what differentiates governance and management in the first place.

Incidentally, the confusion about the chair's role found in corporate governance as well as in nonprofits and units of government is part of the reason why in Policy Governance we often describe the function of the chair as the *chief governance officer*. The CGO designation is more descriptive of the job, since chairing is only one part of the job, and even that the CGO can delegate to someone

> So if you are a CGO, your job is to lead the board, not to lead the CEO.

else. In addition, nonprofit boards variously use *chair* and *president* to describe the chairing role, while some use *president* as a title for their CEO, while corporate boards frequently combine CEO and chair into the same position, further complicating the matter. This habit of confusing title with function led us to use CGO and CEO as definable *functions*, with no regard for what a specific organization chooses to use as titles for these positions.

Boards are usually aware that the CEO works for them and not the other way around, although some boards' behavior seems to indicate otherwise. But many boards are not aware that their chair works for them, acting instead as if the board works for the chair. The Policy Governance board does give authority to the CGO, but authority only to be used in the service of the board and its policy-stated intentions about governance leadership.

Board Control of Board Work

Thus, the board has a CGO to help fine-tune and continually discipline its process, making it possible for the board to take charge of its own work, something that is an almost impossibly tall order without Policy Governance. You may be wondering how the board can decide its own agenda when it is not fully aware of what is going on in the organization and cannot therefore be sure about what should be included. The answer is that the board's agenda is not a "what's going on in the organization" agenda. "What's going on in the organization" refers almost always to operational means and even then of an immediate nature. What's going on in the organization is not the board's work except that the board must make relevant policies at a high level and check in an organized way for compliance. The former is likely already done, and the latter normally requires little time. But to say a proper board agenda is not the continual recounting of operational goings-on many boards have come to expect only says what a proper agenda is *not*. We will deal with what a board agenda should be and how

> So if you are a CGO or CEO, your job is defined by the board, not by the other officer. You can be helpful to each other as much as your help is invited, but as to decisions in your own job, you are obligated to use and be accountable for your own best judgment. You are not beholden to the other officer.

it is generated later in this Guide and more thoroughly in the Carver Policy Governance Guide titled *Implementing Policy Governance and Staying on Track*.

Since the CEO and the CGO have separate leadership jobs, both work for the board and are not themselves related by hierarchy; they are colleagues. There is no reason that they could not exchange information and advice if they choose, but it must be clear that neither has instructive authority over the other, nor the right to evaluate the other's performance.

The CGO: Guardian of the Board's Job

Because the Policy Governance board's job is well defined with specific processes and products spelled out, the "first among equals" role of the CGO is easily derived. The board's group job is clearly delineated in its Governance Process and Board-Management Delegation policies. These policies describe the leadership the board as a body is committed to providing. Typically, the Policy Governance board commits itself to making decisions with a long-term perspective in the interests of owners. It commits itself to prescribing ends but only prohibiting unacceptable operational means. It promises to judge CEO performance only against pre-existing policy criteria. It states in its policies that it will fulfill the needs for frequent self-evaluation and prompt orientation of new board members to its governance process. It has rules about conflicts of interest, transparency, and inappropriate use of board members' positions on the board.

This is all well and good, but you are probably as aware as we are that boards have a long and unfortunate history of making high-flown statements that have little discernible effect on their behavior. In fact, we find that the word *policy* is either scornfully assumed to mean a rigid, bureaucratic device for self-protection or is assumed to mean a rhetorical flourish intended more to look good than cause good.

We have described what board policy means in Policy Governance in other Guides in this series. But even with the more meaningful design of policies for board leadership developed in Policy Governance, these policies would also vanish into history without the commitment of board members to take them seriously and abide by them. The CGO is used in Policy Governance as one element in a board's tools for living up to good intentions (other tools include self-evaluation). The CGO role is therefore to serve the board by leading it, an embodiment of the servant-leadership concept developed by Robert Greenleaf.

The board's role can be described in terms of both process and product—its actions, on one hand, and the value that it adds, on the other. It needs its CGO to assist it to resolve or clarify issues related to both.

> So if you are a CGO, remember it is not your responsibility that the organization works but that the board works at least up to the standards set in its policies. You will find that is job enough. You have only the authority the board chooses to give you, but you must use all you have.

The Board's Job Products

All jobs exist to produce something, not to stay busy at something. So ignoring job activities, let's revisit the description of the minimum, essential, hands-on (nondelegable) job products of a governing board. (We use the terms *job products, values added, outputs,* and *deliverables* to mean the same thing.) The minimal direct outputs or deliverables of a governing board are these three:

1. Informed connection between owners and organizational operators (staff)

2. Written governing policies in the categories respecting the ends-means principle and the descending levels principle

3. Assured organizational performance in compliance with Ends and Executive Limitations policies

Collectively, then, the job is that the board, true to its trustee role on behalf of owners, makes informed decisions as to what the organization's performance should be, then ensures successful performance. Or, condensed even more, the board's overall purpose is *owner-accountable organizational performance.*

> So if you are a board member, keep in mind the job is not just to stay busy with "boardly" activities, no matter how well intended, but to produce certain products that only the board can produce.

It often surprises boards to learn that they have unique job outputs to produce, especially if they have been acting as if the board's role is ceremonial or merely advisory. Policy Governance boards know that their job is real, not advisory and certainly not ceremonial. They also quickly understand that for a group of equals to act as a body and get real work done requires discipline and very good leadership. The nature of the leadership needed is, however, worth careful scrutiny. That is why the CGO has such an important role.

A major contribution by the CGO in leading the board to the accomplishment of its job lies in determining the board's detailed agenda. Here's how it works.

The collection of values added or outputs of any given job is what the person who holds the job is always working on. This is just as true of the board's job as it is of a clerk's. The board's job description at its highest level could therefore be termed the board's "continual agenda," since the board should always be working on producing its unique products. When we know the continual agenda, finding more specific meeting agendas is only a matter of making finer distinctions among these broad outputs.

Of course, the job products listed above do not indicate what should be on the June agenda, for the listed products are broad statements and the items on any one agenda are far more narrowly defined. It is common for the board to further define the policy about its job products by deciding which aspects of those products will be produced in the following year. That would constitute an annual agenda plan.

For example, as to product 1 in the first year, the board could clarify the ownership's identity (not always easy), work out the method of connecting with owners, and develop questions that such interaction will be designed to answer. As to product 2 in the first year, the board could set targets for completion or review of Ends policies. As to product 3 in the first year, the board could identify external resources to monitor certain aspects of performance, choose the remuneration package for the CEO, and if finding a new CEO is contemplated, decide about qualities sought in the new CEO and the search procedures to be used.

An annual agenda plan may not—and in our brief example did not—indicate the precise lineup for the June agenda either. Nevertheless, many boards find it acceptable to stop defining the agenda plan at this point, leaving the "smaller bowl" issues to the CGO's reasonable interpretation. Thus the board's intentions drive its agendas, and through the efforts of the CGO, meeting-by-meeting agendas evolve. The contribution of the CGO in orchestrating the production of job outcomes is invaluable to the board and maintains a clear focus on the board job as separate from that of the CEO.

In this way, the board is in control of its agenda, not needing the CEO to determine what the board should work on. Excellence in governance demands that board meetings be, in truth, the board's meetings, not the CEO's meetings for the board. We will deal further with agenda planning in the Carver Policy Governance Guide titled *Implementing Policy Governance and Staying on Track*.

The Board's Job Process

Individual responsibility is a characteristic with which we are all familiar, even if we differ in how much we demonstrate it. But group responsibility is for most of us uncharted territory, even for persons who've exercised great amounts of individual responsibility. Unfortunately, or fortunately, it is group responsibility that must be exercised if the board is to fulfill its group accountability.

Policy Governance does not create this challenge for boards, but it does often expose the problem. Uncompromisingly, the model maintains that the board, as a group, represents the ownership and bears accountability for the entirety of the organization and that no one has any authority within the board or under the board that the board has not given them, whether intentionally or by default. The board must decide as a group how much authority is to be delegated and to whom. It is critical that the board agree on its delegation method. And the board must act in a way that is consistent with its decisions, for if it does not, it will signal to the rest of the organization not to expect the board to be predictable or consistent.

So the board's job is to produce its values added, its products, but it will not be able to do this without considering some elements of process. Those elements include how diversity can be honored without causing indecisiveness, how a group of equals can demand discipline from each other, how the staff can always be protected from disputes among board members, how good intent is not allowed to deteriorate to being merely rhetorical, and how the board's group job is never impeded by one or two members.

One of the difficulties we regularly encounter with respect to group process arises from the very source one would think is the board's main strength: responsible individuals. It is common for an individual board member to feel that his or her obligation is to act responsibly and to hope everyone else does likewise. The board member is committed to following the rules, perhaps even in an exemplary manner. But being disciplined oneself is only the first step. For group responsibility to work, each member must approach the total group's behavior as his or her own responsibility.

Consequently, any time the board is breaking its own rules, *every* board member who does not raise a hand to object is culpable. If even one board member is unassertive in speaking up or isn't familiar enough with Governance Process and Board-Management Delegation policies to discern that the board is off track, then group responsibility isn't all it should be. We are not suggesting hostile or unpleasant confrontation but merely a reasoned and adult conversation among board members honestly concerned about whether the board can be taken at its word.

We must stress the importance of a board's developing this kind of honest and open process to an extent far beyond what is normally expected. Without leadership that is truly group leadership, the vacuum will be filled by others, such as the CGO, a few assertive board members, or even the CEO. A board unable to lead as a group is also a board unable to stop the vacuum from being filled or to reverse it once begun. Governing an organization, as we previously

So if you are a board member, you must appreciate that responsible and disciplined governance is every board member's responsibility. Most Policy Governance boards have Governance Process policies requiring their members to attend meetings and training, be prepared for meetings, and refrain from undermining the authoritative voice of the board. You not only have to follow these policies yourself, but speak up when others do not follow them.

said about the board, requires that the board first be able to govern itself.

It is in living up to this difficult group responsibility that the Policy Governance board uses the CGO position. But the CGO does not help by substituting for group responsibility; he or she helps by assisting the process to occur. It is important that the CGO not be seen as the only board member with responsibility for board discipline, for that falls on every member's shoulders. However, the CGO is the only member with a gavel. Other board members may and should object to errant board activity, but the CGO is given authority by the group to stop it, as long as the authority wielded is a reasonable interpretation of the board's policies about conduct of its job.

> So if you are a board member, you must remember that the CGO works for the board, not the other way round. But at the same time, you must be aware that you have given this officer the right to make decisions that will keep the board on track with the job it said in its policies that it would do. Allowing the leader to lead is an obligation of the led.

So if all else fails, it is the CGO who must call the board's attention to its having veered off course because that is what Policy Governance boards call on their CGOs to do. If the board has stated that all board members are expected to attend the meetings and trainings and to show up prepared, the CGO must follow up with board members who fail to take these requirements seriously. If the board has said that it will self-evaluate on a regular basis, it is the CGO who must set up or cause to be set up a mechanism for doing this, including deciding how frequent "regular" is. If the board expects its new members to be oriented to Policy Governance, it is the CGO who must see that this occurs, though it is not necessarily the CGO who would provide the orientation. If a board member seems to be forgetting or flouting conflict-of-interest guidelines, the CGO must take action to preserve the ethics of board process. The board has a right to expect its CGO to bring the board's process to the point that it is a reasonable interpretation of what the board has said in policies about its process.

The CGO's job is a curious mixture of leader, servant, enforcer, and planner. If the board goes off course, the CGO must rule on the matter if it is raised by other board members and personally raise the matter if it is not. The CGO's job is not to take the board off the hook for acting as a group but to lead it to do so, a role not easy to take in a group of peers. There is a good deal of social pressure on board members and particularly on CGOs either to sacrifice good process on the altar of being congenial or to give in to the easier route of chair reign. Both result in

> So if you are a CGO, you have been given authority by the board to use on its behalf. Your authority and your responsibility are set forth in board policies. The board charges you to remind it of the rules, enforce them, and fine-tune enactment of its policies so that the board gets its job done as it has defined it. You cannot be either timid or imperious.

board ineffectiveness and proclaim to others such as the staff that the board cannot be relied on to be as disciplined as it demands its staff to be.

The CGO's authority is to choose and act on his or her own reasonable interpretation of all board policies in the two relevant categories. Of course, the policy setting out the CGO role is itself one of those policies. In Exhibit 1 we show a sample "Role of the Chief Governance Officer" policy in the Governance Process category.

> So if you are a CGO, develop your balancing act of rigorously insisting on following your reasonable interpretation of Governance Process and Board-Management Delegation policies but not going beyond them as if you had authority in your own right. You are an instrument of the board, not it of you. Should the board ask you to explain why one of your interpretations should be seen as reasonable, be ready to justify it. Such an interaction isn't personal, just part of maintaining a good system.

Exhibit 1. Policy for the Role of the Chief Governance Officer.

Policy Category: Governance Process

Policy Title: Role of the Chief Governance Officer

The CGO is a specially empowered member of the board who ensures the integrity of the board's process and the completion of its products.

1. The assigned result of the CGO's job is that the board behaves consistently with its own rules and those legitimately imposed on it from outside the organization.

   a. Meeting discussion content will be only those issues that, according to board policy, clearly belong to the board to decide or monitor.

   b. Information that is neither for monitoring performance nor for board decisions will be avoided or minimized and always noted as such.

   c. Deliberation will be fair, open, and thorough, but also timely, orderly, and kept to the point.

2. The authority of the CGO consists in making decisions that fall within topics covered by the board policies on Governance Process and Board-Management Delegation, with the exception of employment or termination of a CEO and where the board specifically delegates portions of this authority to others. The CGO is authorized to use any reasonable interpretation of the provisions in these policies.

   a. The CGO is empowered to chair board meetings with all the commonly accepted power of that position, such as ruling and recognizing.

   b. The CGO has no authority to make decisions about policies created by the board in Ends and Executive Limitations areas. Therefore, the CGO has no authority to supervise, direct, or personally evaluate the CEO.

c. The CGO may represent the board to outside parties in announcing board-stated positions and in stating CGO decisions and interpretations within the area delegated to him or her.

d. The CGO may delegate this authority but remains accountable for its use.

The CEO: Guarantor of Achievement

You may remember that we defined the CEO as first person below the board who has authority over the operational organization and is accountable to the board for the organization's meeting board expectations. The board has the right not to have such a position, but governance then is much more difficult. You can look at the CEO role as summative in the sense that it adds up all the conduct and performance of all staff into one person. From the board's perspective, the CEO is the embodiment of the entire operational organization. When the board delegates to the CEO, it is delegating to the organization. When the board evaluates the CEO, it is evaluating the organization. The clarity and simplicity of the board-CEO relationship is important to accountability.

You've seen that the CEO in Figure 1 appears on the right side of the circle, bounded by board policies on Ends and Executive Limitations. We realize, of course, that inside the right side of the circle, there may be many people. In large organizations, there may be thousands of employees and perhaps even volunteers. But this area, from the board's point of view, must belong to the CEO, since he or she is to be held accountable that the organization accomplishes a reasonable interpretation of the board's Ends and Executive Limitations policies.

Boards that delegate into an operational organization but do not employ a CEO have the task of not only defining the organizational job to be done—that is, defining the Ends and Executive Limitations—but also of deciding on the division of labor among separate people or groups. Such a board would have to check on the various operational units to ensure that each had successfully carried out its part of the work. Boards find this very difficult and rarely do it well. In fact, the main reason for having a CEO is to allow the board to delegate the entire job, including the organizational design, division of labor, and compliance monitoring of organizational units, to a single person whom it can hold accountable for the total.

Most organizations are complex organisms with numerous, separate functions that have to work together like a fine machine if the total of all efforts is to accomplish intended outcomes. The use of a central point of control is essential except in the smallest of groups with the simplest of tasks. (Operating without a CEO imposes additional tasks on the board, such as coordination among operational functions and apportionment of accountability for success and failure.) So while a CEO role may not be needed in some cases, its utility turns into necessity as the size of operational staff increases beyond a handful. From the board's standpoint, there is enormous benefit in having such a central point, because it can then be held accountable for the successful integration of all the parts. The central point in question is a CEO. But a CEO function is an all-or-none proposition; there is no half-CEO, for that would be no CEO at all.

It is clear that no CEO can perform his or her role without substantial authority. You have seen that Policy Governance argues for the board to delegate a great deal of authority to the CEO but to do so safely. The safety of the delegation of authority is important. Without clear board-defined boundaries on CEO authority, the CEO could cause organizational situations that the board would find unacceptable. In addition, the board could, without care, allow the CEO so much authority that the CEO assumes, in effect, the role of the board's superior. On the other hand, delegating insufficient authority to the CEO is self-defeating. As examples, we have seen

> So if you are a board member, your board doesn't have to have a CEO, but you must either have one or not have one. There is no in-between.

CEOs running very large organizations without authority to make purchases over $50,000 and superintendents of huge school systems who by law don't have authority to hire a teacher. The board is accountable for the organization's success, and the CEO has the job of making the organization successful on behalf of the board. The board needs the CEO to be successful, and to underpower the position ultimately damages the board.

In Policy Governance, the authority of the CEO is defined by the "any reasonable interpretation" range of the board's Ends and Executive Limitations policies. The CEO, in other words, has the authority to make decisions within the latitude that the board has established. Boards differ about their values, and so you would expect to see that one board may delegate a broader decision-making range to the CEO while another may be more restrictive.

It is possible, of course, for a board to have too much confidence in its CEO or to give away too much authority. But the only way to fall into that error is for the board to fail to make its judgment of the CEO's performance equal to organizational performance, fail to express the performance requirements it has for the organization, and fail to monitor organizational performance on a routine basis. Avoidance of these failures is built into the Policy Governance model, enabling the board to have a powerful CEO without anxiety.

We have described the CEO position with no reference to membership on the board. That is because there is no need for the CEO to have a board seat that cannot be satisfied another way with less conflict of interest. (Even if laws or regulations prescribe otherwise, it is still a defective practice.) For the CEO to have a vote on the body to which he or she reports damages board independence. The commitment of board members must be to the ownership; the CEO's must be to the board. Just as the board exists to serve the ownership, so the CEO exists to serve the board. When the CEO as board member disagrees with the board vote, these commitments can be at cross-purposes. The reasons often given for having the CEO on the board include the board's wanting the CEO at its meetings and wanting to give the CEO position more prestige. The former does not require board membership, and the latter can be achieved by giving the CEO all the honor a CEO is due at the outset.

The CEO's Work Product: So What Does the CEO Accomplish?

It is important to note that the reason for having a CEO role has nothing to do with the CEO's own personal contribution to the total organizational work. He or she will make certain personal contributions, of course, but his or her accountability is that the entire operational organization produces what it should within the boundaries of prudence and ethics. That is why one of the sample Board-Management Delegation policies we suggest to boards has a statement saying, "The board will view CEO performance as identical to organizational performance, so that organizational accomplishment of board-stated ends and avoidance of board-proscribed means, both reasonably interpreted, will be viewed as successful CEO performance." This is the CEO's job description; the shortest and most easily stated of any in the organization. CEOs, however, would rightly argue that it is not the easiest job to perform.

The board's interest in the CEO's job, then, is not really the CEO's personal job at all but the organization's job. The CEO individually will create for himself or herself a separate job description based on what he or she has retained as CEO work rather than delegated to others. The CEO of one organization may personally handle contracting issues, while the CEO of another may delegate this matter but personally handle aspects of program planning. But that personal job description is of no official concern to the board. The board is not prevented from knowing about the internal delegation system set up by the CEO, but this matter is incidental to the governing job. Certainly the Policy Governance board would never review, appraise, accept, or evaluate the CEO's personal objectives. They are, to the board, irrelevant. All that is relevant is organizational accomplishment of a reasonable interpretation of ends and organizational avoidance of unacceptable means, reasonably interpreted.

The CEO's Work Process: So What Does the CEO Actually Do?

But the CEO must do something him- or herself. So what is the CEO's personal involvement in the total? There is no one answer to this question, since CEOs differ in personal skill sets and inclinations. But there are some aspects of the job that all CEOs must complete. You will remember that the board is the starting point of all authority in the organization and that the CEO has authority only because the board gives it to him or her. Well, other people in the organization working for the CEO need authority too. All CEOs must decide the manner in which other employees (who are directly or indirectly linked to the CEO position) receive their job descriptions and the authority to perform their jobs. Further, the CEO must establish the broad rules that, when met, will allow him or her to demonstrate to the board successful organizational compliance with board policies.

> So if you are a board member, except in relation to Ends and Executive Limitations policies, you really never have to concern yourself officially with what the CEO is doing at all!

The CEO's workflow, from receipt of board policies to submitting monitoring data, might be as shown in Figure 2. The CEO under a Policy Governance board would use board policies as the foundation for the entire organization.

In Figure 2, you can see that before any attempt can be made to comply with board policies, they must be interpreted. This is true when you receive any instruction: you have to decide what it means in order to act on it. Mostly we make our interpretation of everyday instructions or expectations implicitly, but in organizations, these leadership interpretations need to be explicit, for if not, they enlighten and instruct no one. The CEO's interpretations (or operational definitions) of board policies form the broad outline of internal policies and organizational design and they form the basis of the development of plans, including strategic plans and budgets, which are operational means issues. The CEO leads this process of interpretation

Figure 2. The Cycle from Policy to Monitoring.

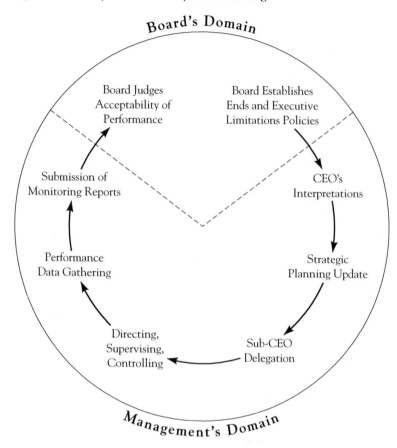

Note: The cycle begins with board establishment of ends and executive limitations policies and terminates with board receipt and judgment of both the reasonableness of the CEO's interpretation and the credibility of performance data.

and planning, but the diagram is not intended to imply that the CEO makes these decisions alone, soliciting no assistance. It would be unusual for a CEO to consider himself or herself competent to complete this step without others' insights. The CEO's accountability to the board, however, is not for getting input but for seeing to it that successful performance occurs. In designing his or her own personal job, the CEO would undoubtedly have to oversee the creation of reasonable interpretations and, later, credible measurement.

We've used the phrase *operational definitions*. This term, not normally familiar to persons outside scientific research, enables a useful bridge from the board's language in Ends and Executive Limitations to the subsequent board ability to ascertain whether a reasonable interpretation of each policy has been fulfilled. Let us illustrate with an example. Suppose we want to know if drinking coffee before driving reduces driver reaction time. A researcher, in order to gather data to solve the question, would first have to settle on concrete definitions of what "drinking coffee" means, what "before" means, and what "reaction time" means. Perhaps, then, one group of drivers that has two cups of fully caffeinated coffee between thirty minutes and one hour prior to driving is presented with an unexpected potential collision situation, and the group's reaction time is expressed in fractions of a second to full depression of a brake pedal. (To simplify, we've left out some components, such as what defines a potential collision and the importance of using the same car for all test subjects.) What the researcher will have produced even before the research is conducted is an operational definition. With this approach to gathering knowledge, anything conceivable is measurable.

Translated to Policy Governance, the CEO would make his or her interpretation of the board's expectations in terms that are themselves measures, just as "drinking coffee" was interpreted to be two cups of fully caffeinated coffee between thirty minutes and one hour prior to driving. That isn't the only reasonable interpretation, but it certainly is one of them. In other words, the "any reasonable interpretation" rule saves the board from going into great detail figuring out workable measures. But the board can rightfully expect that it will later receive measurements that are credible anyway.

In Policy Governance, the CEO's first step after the board has decided on policy wording is to determine operational definitions that can be shown to any fair judge to be reasonable. Then, as demonstrated in Figure 2, after development of interpretations, the CEO conceives of plans to achieve them and can delegate parts of the plans and interpretations to his or her direct reports. These managers in turn delegate to other employees, and so the usual practices of programming, directing, supervising, and controlling proceed. Over time, performance data are collected, possibly prompting midcourse corrections and reinterpretations, and in due course, on the board's schedule, the board is provided with performance data.

Figure 2 shows the connection between board policies and CEO job processes. It is a very busy sequence of often highly technical and professional actions. The coordination of many working parts, varying personalities, and shifting conditions is not easy. But happily, since it has its own work to do, these steps in the CEO job process are not the board's worry. In fact, they come out better if the board stays out of them, as board involvement will contaminate the results for which the CEO is accountable.

We have found that a considerable number of CEOs who work for Policy Governance boards are interested in using some of the principles of Policy Governance in the way they instruct and empower their employees. They tell us that because their boards have defined the ends to be accomplished, they have a clearer than usual sense of the direction in which the organization must be taken. Likewise, the Executive Limitations policies allow the CEO to know exactly the range within which he or she is authorized to act. The result is a sense of real ownership of the job. Moreover, knowing clearly how much authority you have enables more powerful further delegation within the staff, making it possible to take greater advantage of employees' intelligence and creativity. It is hard to powerfully pass on authority to employees if the CEO is not certain what authority he or she has to begin with.

So if you are a board member, you and your colleagues carefully describe successful organizational performance in policies; you subsequently judge whether a reasonable interpretation of those policies has been achieved. But neither you nor the board as a whole is the CEO's management consultant.

The Policy Governance model, by framing the board's prudence and ethical concerns as a fence or corral within which the CEO must stay, thereby creates a free but bounded zone of CEO prerogatives open to CEO and staff creativity, innovation, and agile response to circumstances. While the CEO must prove the organization stays within the free zone, he or she need never explain or get approval for the decisions made within it. Thus it is that for a CEO who wants to perform, boundaries rather than prescriptions are the very essence of freedom.

So some Policy Governance CEOs, knowing their authority and appreciating the "bounded freedom" method of delegation used by the board, delegate to their staff in a similar manner. They instruct their direct reports to see that certain deliverables are produced and that any manner of producing them is authorized except for methods set out as unacceptable. The internal descriptions of unacceptable methods are the CEO's further definitions of board Executive Limitations policies added to whatever additional ones are thought necessary due to purely internal management reasons. As to the deliverables (job outcomes), these may be derived from ends for some managers. Other managers, while they produce internally necessary results, do not produce any part of ends; these include human resources, marketing, and finance.

Avoidable Traps in the Board-CEO Relationship

You may not be surprised to learn that CEOs new to Policy Governance but accustomed to traditional boards can engage in practices with respect to the board that are inconsistent with Policy Governance. Here are some examples.

CEO Asks for Board Approval

In Policy Governance, the board agrees to accept (in effect, it preapproves) all operational means that are not violations of Executive Limitations policies. CEOs who persist in bringing matters to the board for approval tend to drag the board back into decision areas it has already delegated. For example, a CEO with no limitation on

So if you are the CEO, as long as you are operating within the boundaries the board has given you, your decisions are as authoritative as if they were decisions of the board. If you have the right to make a decision, taking it to the board so it will appear more authoritative is a refusal to do your job. CEO leadership, while subordinate to the board's, is leadership certain of its authority and prepared to accept accountability for its use.

authority to design the organizational chart nevertheless may bring his or her plan to the board for approval. Boards should be disciplined enough to recognize and resist this unnecessary request for approval, but don't tempt them! There is no reason to take delegated issues to the board for approval, unless an outside authority such as a regulator or funder requires a formal board approval. In such a case, the item should be on the Required Approvals agenda (explained in the Carver Policy Governance Guide titled *Implementing Policy Governance and Staying on Track*).

CEO Asks for Board Advice

A variant of asking for approval is asking for advice. CEOs and their staff need advice, as do we all, and often there are board members with skills to provide it. It is unlikely that everyone on the board is equally qualified to give advice on a particular topic, but asking individual board members for advice should not be a problem. For one thing, advice, if it is truly advice, can safely be disregarded or turned down with the CEO still accountable for the decisions he or she made. An important side effect of the board's promise to "speak with one voice" with regard to instruction is that advice from individual board members is unambiguously advice, since it cannot possibly be instruction. Under these conditions, board members need not walk on eggshells, for the CEO knows he or she can ignore them.

That point made, we recommend that CEOs wanting advice simply ask persons whose advice is valued, whether they are board members or not. If they are board members, ask for their advice outside board meetings. Asking in a board meeting risks confounding advice and instruction, for it is harder to separate advice from instruction if it appears the whole board is participating in the advising. Sometimes a CEO intentionally asks his or her board to make certain Ends or Executive Limitations policies clearer, yet couches that request as one for advice. Keep in mind that the board has already authorized the CEO to do anything the board has not prohibited and granted the CEO the right to interpret what the board has said as long as it can be shown to be reasonable. The board should never make something "clearer," whether phrased as advice or as an unwritten amendment of a policy. Under the conditions established by Policy Governance, a CEO who seeks advice from the board is usually looking for political cover or doubts that the board meant what it said about executive delegation.

> So if you are the CEO, accepting advice from anyone is OK. But because advice you've accepted from a board member causes you a performance failure does not remove or even lessen your accountability. You are responsible, in effect, for taking bad advice.

CEO Prepares Board Agenda

Traditionally, CEOs have been responsible for much of the content of the board's agenda and have provided information and presentations for the board's edification. To continue to do this after the board has started to use Policy Governance distracts the board from its governance job. Again, the board should be disciplined enough to prevent the CEO taking over its agenda, but testing that discipline is not an appropriate role of the CEO.

CEO Heeds Board Member Instructions

A common issue arises about the one-voice principle. The Policy Governance board is committed to using its authority as a group and is clear that it will not expect the CEO to regard any individual board member input as authoritative. In addition, the board usually has an Executive Limitations policy denying the CEO the freedom

> So if you are the CEO, remember that the leadership required of you involves leading an organization, delegating authority clearly, being unafraid to demand good performance, and taking action when it is not delivered. While we understand that working for a board can be political and that boards can be undisciplined, your obligation to the board is to act as if you are certain that the board means what it says in its policies about its own job and yours.

to "deal with the board in a way that favors some members over others" and to "allow the board to be unaware that in the CEO's opinion, the board is not in compliance with its own policies." Yet there are CEOs who nonetheless treat board member input as if it had instructional authority, failing to exercise their right to reject the input as well as their duty to inform the board if board member incursions persist. We do not mean to imply that the CEO is responsible for keeping the board on track, but keeping the board informed of where it is not on track is not only required but also can be very helpful.

We are often asked if the CEO can be part of the process of board policymaking or if we suggest that the board decide on its policies and then tell the CEO. The question itself surprises us, for we assume the CEO to be a valuable information resource. What a waste it would be for the CEO's information to be untapped by the board. We encourage the board to use the CEO and anyone else with relevant information as a resource when making policies. The CEO can describe the implications of the board's making this or that policy and can alert the board to the possibility of either overreaching or being unneces-

> So if you are the CEO, be ready to provide relevant information about decisions that the board is making. Understand that the board has the right to make decisions you don't like. Your objections should be heard but are not decisive. You will be given a great deal of authority, but you work for the board, not the other way round.

sarily timid with respect to the ambition expressed in its policies. There is no reason to exclude the CEO from the board's process, as long as the respective roles are clear. The board decides its policies on behalf of the owners, not on behalf of the CEO. The CEO has no right to make board policies but should be encouraged to have input into board deliberations about them.

Policy Governance boards are usually concerned that their policies may become irrelevant or outdated because of changes they are not aware of. They recognize that they may have made policies that over time conflict with each other. In these instances, they usually make an Executive Limitations policy describing as unacceptable the CEO's failure to keep them informed of such changes. The CEO is therefore viewed as an important resource in helping the board keep its policies current. This is the board's responsibility but one with which the CEO is specifically required to help.

> So if you are the CEO, you have an important role as adviser to the board. You are required to inform the board if its policies are unrealistic or unachievable. Remember that if you are aware of such problems, the board needs to be informed as soon as possible. Telling the board at monitoring time that the organization is out of compliance with a policy because there was a problem with the policy itself is late and perhaps disingenuous.

The Policy Governance board may have as many delegatees as it wishes. But it will be wise to keep the number to a minimum, since each requires board time and study to charge with responsibilities and to monitor. We recommend a CGO to help the board be a responsible group and a CEO to produce organizational effectiveness, prudence, and ethics. Committees can be added, and individual assignments can be made to board members. But the CGO and CEO are the really important officers for successful governance and management. The jobs are separable, not ever needing to be in conflict or overlap.

Conclusion

In this Guide, we have described and distinguished the two key roles of Chief Executive Officer and Chief Governance Officer. The principles of Policy Governance enable these officers to be given non-overlapping, authoritative roles, both reporting to the board.

About the Authors

John Carver is internationally known as the creator of the breakthrough in board leadership called the Policy Governance model and is the best-selling author of *Boards That Make a Difference* (1990, 1997, 2006). He is co-editor (with his wife, Miriam Carver) of the bimonthly periodical *Board Leadership*, author of over 180 articles published in nine countries, and author or co-author of six books. For over thirty years, he has worked internationally with governing boards, his principal practice being in the United States and Canada. Dr. Carver is an editorial review board member of *Corporate Governance: An International Review*, adjunct professor in the University of Georgia Institute for Nonprofit Organizations, and formerly adjunct professor in York University's Schulich School of Business.

Miriam Carver is a Policy Governance author and consultant. She has authored or co-authored over forty articles on the Policy Governance model and co-authored three books, including *Reinventing Your Board* and *The Board Member's Playbook*. She has worked with the boards of nonprofit, corporate, governmental, and cooperative organizations on four continents. Ms. Carver is the co-editor of the bimonthly periodical *Board Leadership* and, with John Carver, trains consultants in the theory and implementation of Policy Governance in the Policy Governance Academy.

John Carver can be reached at P. O. Box 13007, Atlanta, Georgia 30324-0007. Phone 404-728-9444; email johncarver@carvergover nance.com.

Miriam Carver can be reached at P. O. Box 13849, Atlanta, Georgia 30324-0849. Phone 404-728-0091; email miriamcarver@carver governance.com.

Notes

Printed and bound by CPI Group (UK) Ltd, Croydon, CR0 4YY